HOMES IN THE HEAVENS

HOMES IN THE HEAVENS

SIMON BENTLEY

WHITE EAGLE PUBLISHING TRUST
NEW LANDS · LISS · HAMPSHIRE · ENGLAND

First published June 2009

© *Copyright, The White Eagle Publishing Trust, 2009*

Cataloguing-in-Publication Data
A catalogue record for this publication is available
from the British Library

ISBN 978-0-85487-209-1

Set in Baskerville by publishink, info@publishink.co.uk
Printed in China by Artical Printing

CONTENTS

INTRODUCTION

Right back in the dark days of the Second World War, Joan Hodgson wrote a series of articles about the spiritual significance of the twelve signs of the zodiac in the White Eagle Lodge magazine, *Angelus*. In 1943, the articles were brought together as a book and published under the title *Wisdom In The Stars*. It has stayed in print ever since, and remains a classic text on the signs.

This book is designed to be a companion to it, this time considering the twelve houses of the horoscope rather than the signs. It, too, started life as a series of articles in the Lodge magazine, by then renamed *Stella Polaris*. It is hoped that it will be as helpful to readers as its predecessor, and also that it will enjoy the same longevity!

Nearly everyone knows which sign of the zodiac was occupied by the Sun when they were born, as it is relatively easy to ascertain from the birthday. Working out which house the Sun was in when you were born is a little more difficult, but well worth doing to enable you to get the most out of this book. Instructions are given in the appendix.

Whereas the position of the Sun in the zodiac indicates the basic soul lesson and work of the life, as described in *Wisdom In The Stars*, its position in the houses tells the astrologer in which area of life that lesson and work will mainly manifest. The houses govern the external manifestation of the forces represented by the planets and signs. If you study first your Sun sign in *Wisdom In The Stars*, and then your Sun house in this book, together they should give you a fuller picture of the basic purposes behind your current life. However, every chapter of both books will be of interest, as we probably all know at least one person with the Sun in each of the twelve signs and twelve houses!

THE HOUSES EXPLAINED

Almost everyone is aware of the signs of the zodiac. Their names are well known, even if mainly because of the Sun-sign columns in newspapers and magazines, and we nearly all know what our Sun sign is from the date of our birthday. For many people, that is the sum total of their astrological knowledge, but it is important knowledge because the position of the Sun reveals much about the fundamental purposes of the life. Knowing in which house of the horoscope the Sun is placed gives us a further insight into these purposes.

What does the word 'home' mean to you? Of all the words and concepts in almost any language, this is one of the most evocative. It makes us think of our roots, the place where we live and, we hope, our anchor in life, a place of security from which we can emerge to face the outside world. Home implies familiar surroundings and companions, the possessions and routines of one's personal life. We all carry with us that concept of home: wherever life takes us, like it or not, home is where we belong.

For most of us, home is to be found in a house of some sort. We tend to live in one particular house, but we also visit others in the course of life. We enjoy visiting some more than others; feel more comfortable in some than in others. We do different things, perform in different ways. At the same time, this does not change our essential selves or our place in life.

From the viewpoint of the astrologer, it is the same with the Sun, Moon and planets in the so-called houses of the horoscope. They may be placed in particular houses at birth, but as the life proceeds they will 'visit' others by 'progression', as it is called. They are more 'comfortable' in some houses than in others. The twelve houses are, in their way, just as important as the signs, indicating as they do the areas of life in which the influences of the planets and signs actually manifest in the conditions of day-to-day life.

Physically, the twelve houses, rather than being composed of stars or constellations, are vast segments of the heavens. Just as some fruit, such as oranges, consist of a number of segments that make up the whole, so the heavens can be viewed as comprising twelve great segments of sky. These segments are determined not by the stars or planets, although they obviously occupy them, but by your view of the heavens from where you are placed (see Figure 1).

2

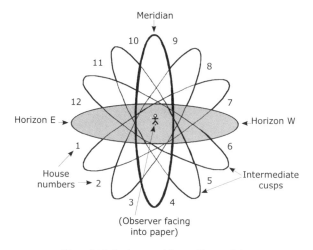

Figure 1: The horizon, meridian and house circles

The heavens can be divided in various ways for conven-
ience of observation and understanding, but the most
basic division is the most obvious: half the sky is visible
above you, the other half invisible beneath your feet.
The boundary between the two is the horizon, the point
where earth and sky appear to meet. In terms of the astrological houses, numbers one to six are beneath your
feet, numbers seven to twelve in the visible sky. The first
six have more to do with areas of life that are more

3

basic and personal, more immediate and somewhat more limited in scope; the second six with those areas that involve others and the wider world, areas that require one to open out one's vision and consciousness to issues of more general significance.

The second most important division is that created by the circle that passes vertically from right above your head through due north in one direction and due south in the other down to the point of the heavens directly beneath your feet. Astronomers know this circle as the *meridian*, a word derived from Latin and meaning 'midday', because it is midday when the Sun crosses that line in its daytime passage across the sky. The first three and last three of the twelve houses are placed on the eastern side of this circle, in the 'rising' half of the heavens, while houses four to nine are placed in the western, 'setting', half. The first group has more to do with the life conditions we actively pursue for ourselves; the second with conditions that tend to come to us, where we play a more passive role. These interpretations regarding the major divisions must be taken as very generalized, but can be seen to apply particularly when someone has most of the planets in one particular half (or even quadrant) of the sky.

The angles and the cusps of the houses

The circles that create these two major divisions in the heavens, the horizon and the meridian, form a great three-dimensional cross, as it were, dividing the heavens into four quadrants, each comprising three of the twelve houses. The four 'dividing lines' – *angles* in astrological terminology – mark four important points that have special significance and are connected with the first of each group of three houses. The most important of these angles is the one defined by the eastern horizon, the point where heavenly bodies rise. This is called the *ascendant*. Just as in physical terms a body such as the Sun becomes visible as it crosses this line, so in astrological terms the ascendant is the point at which what is in the rest of the horoscope becomes visible. It represents the outer self, the face we present to the world and which the casual acquaintance most easily recognizes. It also determines the first house in the horoscope, the house of the personality, the self, the physical body and the general outlook on life.

The angle defined by the upper portion of the meridian is physically the point at which heavenly bodies reach their highest point in the sky. Astrologically this is called the *mid-heaven* or the MC (*medium caelum* – the middle of the sky). It determines the tenth house in the horoscope, which has much to do with our achieve-

5

ment in the outside world, especially with regard to career or vocation.

Opposite the ascendant is the *descendant*, the setting point on the western horizon. This determines the seventh house and, being opposite the first, is associated with experience that comes through others rather than from self. For example, marriage comes under this house.

Opposite the mid-heaven is the nadir point or IC (*imum caelum* – the bottom of the sky), at which heavenly bodies reach their lowest point beneath our feet. This determines the fourth house and, just as the tenth house denotes achievement in the outer world, the public life as it were, the fourth, opposite to it, denotes the private life, matters of home and family.

Technically, these angles are also the *cusps* of the first, tenth, seventh and fourth houses respectively. However, all the houses have cusps, not just these four most important ones. Most readers will have met the term before, but maybe only with reference to the boundaries between the zodiac signs – people born with the Sun close to the border between two signs tend to speak of themselves as being born 'on the cusp'. In terms of the houses, while in some way the cusps are boundary lines between the houses, they are also sensitive points – any body placed on a cusp is rendered strong. For the purposes of using this book, however, it is only necessary to consider the cusps in their role as boundary lines.

House division

Readers may wonder how the cusps of the intermediate houses are determined, and this has always been a matter of controversy among astrologers. The overall idea is to have the sky divided into twelve equal segments, but there are many different ways of doing this, according to what is kept equal. The exact technical nature of the different house systems need not concern us here, but the system we use is termed *topocentric*, so when you use the appendix to find your solar house position, it is in this system that the answer is determined. You don't need to remember this, however!

The symbolism of the houses

It is usual to write or print a horoscope chart on to a circular form, a wheel if you will, in which each of the house cusps appears like a spoke of that wheel (Figure 2). The horizon line across the middle, however, is often doubled or thickened to emphasize its importance. The meridian line from top to bottom is also thickened. These two can be seen to form a cross within the circle of the wheel, a perfect symbol in itself of what incarnation means. The circle is the symbol of spirit, the cross

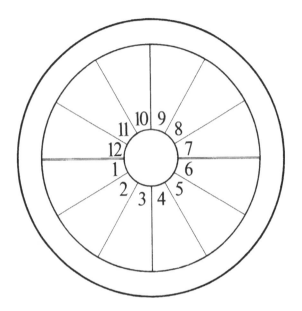

Figure 2: Blank chart wheel

the symbol of matter, so the very chart itself demonstrates, in its basic construction, the symbolism of spirit incarnating in matter.

You may have wondered why there are twelve houses – and twelve signs, of course, for that matter – rather than, say, ten or eleven or thirteen or fourteen. The answer lies in the very symbolism mentioned above. Multiply three, the number of spirit, by four, the number of matter, and you get twelve. Therefore there are twelve 'expressions', if you like, of what happens when spirit (three) incarnates in matter (four). Physically, the houses are but great segments of the heavens, vast cosmic spaces; spiritually, however, they show the meeting point between spiritual intention and physical life that results in day-to-day circumstance and experience.

It has sometimes been said, especially in astrology textbooks, that the zodiac signs have to do with character, and the houses with destiny. While there is a degree of truth in this, it is not entirely correct. It is better to consider the signs to be representative of the tasks the soul has to perform in order to reach perfection, rather like the labours of Hercules, with which the signs have frequently been linked, while the houses indicate the manner in which such tasks are actually performed.

Looked at in this light, the distinction between the signs and the houses in terms of character and destiny is less clear-cut. What is not in doubt is that the houses play an essential role in our understanding of day-to-day life.

9

The Sun in the houses

In this book, you can learn about the nature of each of the twelve houses, particularly the one in which your Sun is placed. However, remember, too, that every heavenly body will occupy some house or other, so if you feel a house description fits your life especially well, but it is not the one your Sun is in, it is likely that it is occupied by other important bodies. The significance of the one that the Sun does occupy, irrespective of whether other things are there too, is that it shows the area of life in which the main 'soul lesson', the main task of life at the deepest level, is being acted out. Other emphasized houses can show areas of life that are especially difficult or especially congenial, or that simply occupy a lot of time and attention. Ultimately, while everything in the horoscope matters, the Sun is paramount.

THE FIRST HOUSE

Of all the twelve houses, the first is the most important. Its 'cusp' (see previous chapter) is the ascendant, or rising degree – the point of the zodiac on the eastern horizon at birth. It is at this point that heavenly bodies become physically manifest, i.e. they rise, and so become visible. The same is true astrologically speaking, in the sense that all the other features of the horoscope have to manifest in the outer world through the medium of the ascendant: its role is therefore as a kind of filter or lens that focuses the personality and projects it into the outside world, making it almost as important, in its way, as the Sun.

Just as the Sun is physically at the heart of the solar system, so in the horoscope the Sun represents the spirit, the 'spark of the divine' that is found at the heart of each one of us. It therefore also indicates to the astrologer the basic motivation behind the life. However, the ascendant, showing as it does the face we present to the world – in computer-speak we might say the 'interface' between the soul and the material world – represents the manner in which we express that motivation, and the way in which the world presents itself to us.

Thus the first house and its cusp, the ascendant, indicate to the astrologer the overall nature of the personality, that part of the much greater higher self that has been, as it were, projected into incarnation. It represents the part of that greater self that we can actually perceive.

The Sun and/or planets in the first house, especially if close to the ascendant, affect the personality very strongly. The qualities associated with such planets or with the sign(s) they occupy are brought out into the external life; they will tend to be noticed by others more than they would in other parts of the horoscope. Any disharmony between such a planet and the sign it is in, or between the planet and the sign on the ascendant, has a pronounced effect on the entire life and the soul's outlook upon it. Many of the conflicts within a personality stem primarily from a difference between the ascendant sign, or first-house conditions, and what is in the rest of the horoscope. Many useful lessons are learned, and much karma faced, through such differences – so simple, but so far-reaching in their effects.

The physical body itself is also denoted by the first house, as it is, of course, the part of us that is literally seen by others. The various different signs on the cusp result in differing types of physical appearance, although these are, in their turn, modified by the influence of any planets in the house and, sometimes, other factors elsewhere in the horoscope. Skilled astrologers can often recognize someone's rising sign from his or her appearance. That appearance, as with basic personality traits, has a profound effect on the life. So much depends on what we look like, even though it shouldn't; one's appearance is radically important.

As a corollary to this, the first house also indicates the general health and well-being, and the outlook on and attitude to life. All these factors are part of what, for want of a better word, we call the 'self'. The first is the house of the self, the house of one's identity. This is borne out by a fact that is well known to astrologers: a strongly emphasized first house often indicates that a search for or establishment of identity is an important part of the life experience.

The 'soul intention' meets, in the first house, the most basic areas of physical life: the need for a physical body and the need for a personality through which to express on the physical plane something of the nature of the higher self. It could be said that the first house is the symbolic representation of the soul's need to manifest and to experience. This readily links it with the first sign of the zodiac, Aries, and its ruler, Mars. In Aries, the soul's task is to overcome self; the first house shows the manner in which self is met, expressed and handled. Mars always seeks manifestation, to bring things into being, for its symbol shows the spirit struggling to express itself through matter. The first house shows the conditions in physical life associated with that expression.

The Sun in the first house

If you have the Sun in the first house, you have probably found that self-expression is a particularly significant issue in your life. This does not mean it is necessarily easy or difficult, but rather that it matters a lot! Sometimes, the most important thing in life is to find out who you are, and, although it might take a long time, it can be a very rewarding process.

Expressing the inner self (Sun) outwardly (first house/ascendant) is what the soul really most wants to do, however hard it might prove to be; according to the sign of the zodiac involved, this takes place in various ways. For example, if you have the Sun in a water sign (Cancer, Scorpio, Pisces), emotional expression will be highlighted; if in an air sign (Gemini, Libra, Aquarius), mental expression and verbal and written communication will matter more. If you have the Sun in an earth sign (Taurus, Virgo, Capricorn), expression in practical or material terms is what is called forth; and if it is in a fire sign (Aries, Leo, Sagittarius), it could once again be emotional, and almost always also creative and/or inspirational.

The first house is quite a challenging position for the Sun, although technically the Sun is comfortable there, because it shows that the soul is setting itself the task of 'shining forth' its very essence into outer life. With, say, a fire sign involved, this is usually fine, but if the Sun is in water, for example, the need to do this might not sit happily with the sensitivity and reticence usually associated with water. Nevertheless, shine forth it will, even in the midst of emotional pain and difficulty as well as joy. The first house is the house that says 'I am', whatever that might demand either of the person him- or herself, or of life generally. Because of this, Sun in the first house can sometimes seem to denote a rather egocentric personality, but, in a way, you could say that it is meant to be.

THE SECOND HOUSE

The first house is followed by the second, which is traditionally recognized by many as the 'money' house. While financial issues are linked with the second house, this is a far from adequate description. The first house, as we have seen, is the house of the self; the second is the house that denotes the resources available to the self. This needs to be interpreted in its widest possible sense. 'Resources' can be available at many different levels, and money is but one of them: emotional, mental and spiritual talents and gifts can be indicated by this house.

However, it is inevitably to money that most people's thoughts turn when the second house is under consideration. It is a major force in life, both in what it enables and what lack of it prevents. Most of us have little understanding of its true significance and role in human evolution, although the well known saying 'money is power' holds a great deal of truth that is not difficult to recognize.

Occultists often say that money is concretized energy; this, too, is true. Perhaps a better way to see it, however, is as symbolic of service. We earn money by giving service – to people, to companies and organizations, to the world in general – so what we earn is symbolic of the service we have given. On the other side of the equation, when we spend money, we are acquiring service from others – the farmer who grew our food, the people who built our house, made our furniture, those who entertained us, and so on.

Of course, the situation does not always seem as simple as this: some are born with money, it seems, whereas others work hard but have none. However, we can be sure that the law of karma determines that over the course of our many incarnations this 'concretized power' or service is distributed with exact justice.

Financial issues will indeed often be prominent in the lives of those with the second house emphasized. Quite often, a strong second house leads to a financial career, such as banking or accountancy. Careers involving building are also common, such as architecture, interior design, and the manufacture of furniture, as well as careers that deal with land and property, such

17

as estate agency, agriculture, horticulture, landscaping, estate management, and so on.

As indicated earlier, the second house is connected not just with money, but also with resources of all kinds. Sometimes this can mean other physical resources, such as crops and commodities; sometimes it can mean metaphorical or abstract resources, the talents and gifts one has available to use in the life. If the first house is about what you are, the second is about what you have, what is at your disposal in the current life.

Just as the first house is linked with the first sign of the zodiac, Aries, and its ruler Mars, so the second house is linked with the second sign, Taurus, and its ruler Venus. Taurus teaches the soul about the resources that can be won and used through service; the second house shows the circumstances surrounding them and the ways in which this is likely to happen.

In order to gain a true understanding of the second house, it is necessary to remember that the spiritual task associated with the second sign, Taurus, is the building of the 'soul temple', the habitation of the soul on the inner planes. Many spiritual teachers talk of the need to perfect the 'rough ashlar' of the personality into the true and perfect building block for that soul temple. In order to perform a task of building at the physical level, one naturally needs supplies of building materials, but one also needs the tools, the skills and abilities to use those materials, otherwise they will simply go to waste. In the second house, we can see the materials that are available for furthering the grand process that is the building of the soul temple. These will include the tools available to the soul, plus the skills it already possesses and can use in the current life.

Thus the second house does indeed show one's material resources, as these correspond at the earthly level to skills or gifts developed and earned at other levels in previous experiences, but above and beyond that, it shows the resources of personality, of mind and spirit, that the soul has brought back into incarnation. However, in reality, as we are often told, no one possesses anything. All belongs to the divine source from which we came. So, ultimately, experiences involving this house, the house of resources, teach us that the most important resources of all are, of course, the love, wisdom and power of God, which make all things possible.

The Sun in the second house

If you have the Sun in the second house, you are likely to have found that, whatever else is happening in your life, your feet tend to be firmly anchored by material considerations, whether you like it or not. You might be involved in one of the careers mentioned earlier; if not, you may be working privately with material issues, responsibilities involving resources, how to use them more effectively, or how to develop a better attitude towards them.

There is often an urge to build or create in some way, though this is as likely to be abstract as physical. Whereas the first house tends to concentrate on the expression of self, the second focuses on being able to see concrete results from one's efforts. The symbol of Venus, ruler of Taurus and therefore the 'natural' ruler of the second house, is the circle, representing spirit, above the cross, representing matter, so there is always an urge (whether recognized or not) to express the beauty of spirit in the outer life in some way.

Sun in the second sometimes brings lessons concerning conservation of energy, though the energy may take many forms. It can be as basic as controlling one's spending, or learning to be more open-handed with resources; at other times, it works out through learning to use emotional or mental resources more effectively or generously. Appreciating the gifts and talents of others is also part of the experience – for example, talent scouts might have something important in the second house as their career involves looking for metaphorical 'resources' in the gifts and talents of the people they spot, and working out how they can be used to best advantage.

THE THIRD HOUSE

Having considered the first two houses, the houses of the self and resources, we come now to the third. While the first house shows how we seek to express ourselves through a physical body and personality, and the second the resources available to us to help us in that ongoing process, the third house denotes the circumstances around our ability to think and to communicate.

The eternal spark, that spirit of God that is within us all, that has, through the first house, drawn to itself a body through which to manifest, and through the second, the resources to maintain that body, finds, through the third, a way of expressing its essence to affect everyday life through the medium of the mind. The mind is the crucial link between spirit, on the one hand, and personality and body on the other; like the mythical Hermes, it is the messenger winging its way between the gods and humanity, maintaining the all-important link between spirit and matter. Spirit desires to act upon matter, but cannot do so without the agency of mind, however basic or complicated that agency may be.

Thus the third house is to be found operating in two main areas of life: first, in anything involving the mind in the most general and broad sense; and second, in many situations in which links between people are established, whether they be temporary or permanent. The third house is therefore the house that shows the conditions surrounding the day-to-day exercise of our minds, in speech and writing, education, communication, study and so on. It also has very general social connotations, especially with regard to the most casual and taken-for-granted interactions of daily life. This makes it very important, despite its apparently obscure position near the foot of the horoscope. Few things in life can be accomplished entirely alone or without mental exercise, so the experiences of this house teach us to use our minds, and that we all need others in our evolutionary journey.

It has often been said that 'as a man thinks, so he becomes'. This being so, the importance of the third house cannot be overemphasized, since the experiences it encompasses, however trivial they may sometimes be, are all opportunities to exercise that mind and therefore to initiate change in ourselves, whatever else may be accomplished at the same time. Through our minds, we can act upon our own personalities, our own behaviour; we can become that all-important observer of our own unfolding life, watching, assessing, and seeing where changes need to be made.

For most of us, this process is happening all the time and we rarely notice it, except when we deliberately and consciously stand back to do so. However, think back over your own life and you will soon realize how powerful the effect of your mind can be. The most obvious example is provided by one's schooldays. Education is acknowledged by all as profoundly important. Why? Because it helps us to understand the world into which we have incarnated and, having understood it, to affect it as well as being affected by it. The truly educated person changes his or her internal world all the time: every thought brings about a modification, another step of growth.

The third may therefore also be regarded as the house of civilization, again in a very broad sense, and it is the area of the horoscope associated with all those conveniences of modern life that we tend to take for granted. In national horoscopes and in horary astrology (the use of astrology to answer specific questions), the infrastructure that supports civilized life is shown by this house, everything that keeps day-to-day existence going.

The third house is linked with the third sign, Gemini, the sign of the Twins. Interaction between people is implicit in that symbol, and this is reflected in the third house in that it indicates our relations with others generally, most of all those we have to live with whether we like it or not, such as our siblings, our peer group at school, or, later on, those involved in our daily routines. The human soul learns much through these 'ordinary' relationships.

The planetary ruler of both sign and house is Mercury, the winged messenger, which symbolizes the power of the mind and the communicative faculty. Through the agency of Mercury, the third house enables the spirit of humanity to work upon the conditions of the world it finds itself in. Mostly imperceptibly, this brings about the change and progress that are intrinsic to life and, ultimately, enable an ever more perfect expression of that spirit in the outer life.

The Sun in the third house

If you have the Sun in the third house, one thing you will almost certainly have found is that life is causing you to appreciate the significance of the apparently trivial event, interaction, word or activity. Communication is almost always an important issue in the life, whether this is recognized consciously or not. You may find yourself involved in work in which communication is particularly important, and the most ordinary and fleeting interactions with others often prove significant: a smile or a couple of kind words to the person who serves you in a café, whom you pass in the street, whom you buy your groceries from, could make all the difference to him or her at that moment. Sooner or later, third-house experience nearly always demonstrates the power of the word, spoken or written, for both good and ill.

Typical careers for Sun in the third are education, printing, any kind of work as an agent or go-between, information technology, and work for public utilities or other infrastructure such as roads, railways and so on. Travel of a routine kind comes under this house, so with the Sun here there is often a tendency for that to be a major part of life, or for the life to be in some way connected with travel facilities.

In the personal life, relationships with siblings are often particularly significant, and there is almost always a desire to keep family members in touch with one another, even, or perhaps especially, when there are difficulties involved. The position is, paradoxically, also sometimes a very shy one; this tends to be due to karma involving the use of speech or writing that has left the soul feeling fearful or nervous about the effect of its words.

This position often indicates very variable moods – the word 'mercurial' being appropriate – and sometimes a definite need to cultivate the habit of always seeing the best in others and in situations, and 'looking on the bright side'. The moods can often be too heavily influenced by every tiny occurrence, so that there is a need deliberately to develop an attitude that treats happenings proportionately and maintains a sensible perspective on life. Over-reaction is common, but to be avoided. The mature soul with this position registers everything, but does not allow its equilibrium to be disturbed.

THE FOURTH HOUSE

At first sight, the fourth house is very different in tone from the third. However, while this is true in many ways, the two houses do share one important factor: in different ways, both affect our taken-for-granted relationships with others. The fourth is very much the house of home and family, being associated with the sign of Cancer and its ruler the Moon, symbolic of the Divine Mother. Third- and fourth-house experience both draw attention to family relationships, the third through the desire to keep lines of communication open, the fourth through ties of emotion and dependency. Being the house of home and family, the fourth indicates many of the conditions surrounding our parents and our upbringing. Later in life, it denotes the circumstances surrounding the family life we make for ourselves as adults. Our physical domestic surroundings are also denoted by this house.

All of us, whether we like it or not, are profoundly affected by our origins, our ancestry, our 'roots'. These can help or hinder our progress in life, and are almost invariably deeply karmic. The Moon, being so closely associated with the mother principle, has much to do with 'where we come from' in every sense. This therefore means not only physical heredity, but also incarnational heredity, and those habits and patterns of behaviour that have become ingrained. These tend to manifest most in the privacy of the domestic life: it is here, more than in any other area of life, that habits are both made and broken.

To understand the fourth house, simply remember the word 'parent' and everything it means to you. All those things find a place in that house. Thus issues of caring, nurturing, protection and security are housed here, as are the issues that come to the fore when we ourselves have the responsibility of providing these things for others. The example we set our children is as much influenced by the fourth house as was the example our parents set us. Fourth-house experience ultimately draws forth from us all those Divine Mother qualities of caring, compassion and quiet authority that act as a guide through life and, when things go wrong, become those 'everlasting arms' of God that support every one of us.

However, the house also works at another level, representing the spiritual 'home' that we all withdraw to, whether consciously or unconsciously, when we need a refuge. This may be a place created in our imagination, for example, but whatever form it takes it is almost always a source of inner, psychological sustenance and support. A strong fourth house can denote quite an introspective character for this reason, as the inner life is often more congenial than the outer, everyday life. There can be a tendency to spend a lot of time facing problems internally, resolving conflict and finding peace, while on the surface few would realize anything was going on other than what they see.

Spiritual practices such as meditation often come naturally to fourth-house people, and they can be drawn to contemplative ways of life, although they are not usually reclusive (which is more associated with the twelfth house). Sensitivity and shyness are common, but there is not usually any lack of practicality or common sense.

The Sun in the fourth house

If you have the Sun in the fourth house, like it or not, domestic and family matters will tend to dominate your life. This can manifest in various ways. There can be heavy family responsibilities, or challenges in relationships within the family circle, for example. Family history or ancestry may be a significant factor in your life, or family land, property or business.

The home life in early years can be a secure foundation on which the rest of the life is built, or, according to karma, it might be something the soul has to strive to grow away from in order to develop a new concept of 'home' for itself, or to leave behind family bonds that are restrictive or unhealthy.

The fourth-house position often draws the soul to work that involves, or takes place in, people's homes – it is a common position for doctors or interior designers, for example, as well as those who take on routine domestic work for their living. Work that involves the provision of those things that keep us nurtured and secure is also common, such as food and crops, clothing (as a necessity rather than as fashion), and childcare, as is care of the elderly as the fourth house governs the final stages of life as well as the early years.

The fourth-house experience is fundamentally about two things: first, it is about bringing forth from the soul the 'mother' qualities of caring, nurturing and kindness; and second, it is about the soul's search for its real, inner home, that place of peace that lies deep within us all and that, sooner or later, we all need to learn to contact.

Distressing and problematic domestic situations are often the spur the soul needs to look inwards for the real security that comes from contact with its spiritual roots, rather than continually seeking that security in other people or external situations.

While useful to everyone, the practice of meditation, which facilitates that inner contact, is of special significance to the fourth-house individual, for whom the inner search for peace and security is so important. The one who has already found it can indeed be 'mother' to all, radiating a gentle and peaceful strength upon which others can always rely, whatever their troubles.

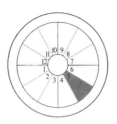

THE FIFTH HOUSE

One of the things that we learn most about in our experiences with home and family (associated with the
fourth house), is the great need all humans have both
to love and be loved. This is the province of the next
house, the fifth. The associated sign is Leo, whose ruler
is the Sun, so in this house we meet all those experiences
that come from the heart, in every sense.

The Sun is symbolic of God the Father, and thus of
the divine light that animates all life: it is the spark of
divinity that lies buried within every one of us. The fifth
house is all about those things that enable the true expression of that divine nature. Fifth-house experiences
put us intimately in touch with this, our 'real' self, aiding
the expression of love in our lives. Ultimately, the love
in question is the love that God has for creation, divine
love, although our ability to realize and express this usu-

ally has to be learned through circumstances related to love at a more human level.

All matters of love are therefore linked with this house, particularly those experiences we still quaintly refer to as 'love affairs'. However, anything that awakens the heart in some way and stimulates its expression is normally a fifth-house matter. Above all, this means all forms of creativity, because true creation comes from that heart-impulse.

Love is the motivating force behind all creation and all that is good and worthwhile. The urge to create can and does take innumerable forms; a strong fifth house in a natal chart will usually denote much creativity, although whether it will be afforded expression depends partly on other factors in the horoscope.

Children are traditionally associated with the fifth house for two main reasons. First, they are the most obvious product of our creativity; second, they stimulate the love-aspect in the human personality, touching our hearts in a way that perhaps nothing else could.

Because the heart is the centre and core of the self, just as the Sun is the central body in the solar system, giving light and life, any experience that puts us at the centre of something is also related to the fifth house. Thus leaders of many kinds and those who 'shine' in a metaphorical sense often have some fifth-house emphasis. Quite frequently, a strong fifth can take a soul on to the stage, whether literally, in a dramatic career, or metaphorically, as for one who has to play a part in local, national or world affairs on the public 'stage'. Our ability to 'lead' ourselves, to take charge of all the various aspects of our being, is also related to the fifth house, which, perhaps surprisingly until you see the connection here, has much to do with our ability for, and manner of applying, self-discipline. To give a simple example, Neptune in the fifth house may denote one who is tempted to indulge in various forms of escapism, but it could equally well indicate someone who works hard to improve his or her physical fitness through swimming.

The fifth is also the house of joy, because joy, too, comes from the heart. Thus pleasure and leisure activities are found here, such as entertainment, sport and so on. All in all, this house is associated with all circumstances and experiences that help us to realize our innate divinity, showing us how, one day, we too may become 'gods' in our own right.

The Sun in the fifth house

If you have the Sun in the fifth house, whatever is going on in the rest of the horoscope you will meet experiences that help to bring out the 'heart' in you and, having done that, to use that love, warmth and creativity wisely. Thus, in personality terms, the two most common manifestations of this position are the soul who is full of love, joy and spontaneity but is learning more about how to use them sensibly, and the soul who desires to develop these qualities, perhaps after a series of lives that have emphasized the mind at the expense of the heart, for example.

Important experiences of human love are almost always part of the life. With the first type of soul, the heart often rules the head, with widely varying consequences! With the second type, there is generally an awakening process, which can be sudden or gradual according to general horoscopic conditions, and manifests itself in increasing warmth and a 'loosening' of the personality.

Relationships with children are apt to be particularly significant. Indeed, quite apart from their role in the individual's private life, this position can lead to work with children; thus teachers sometimes have this position. This does not necessarily only mean children in the physical sense. Sometimes the fifth-house person is led to work with the young in soul, whatever their physical age may be, giving them the guidance and authority that befits the house associated with Leo, the father figure.

Very commonly, the Sun in the fifth takes people into the creative, artistic sphere, since ultimately the fifth is about self-expression. This may be in art, music, dance or drama, but whatever the field in which it manifests, it is about the sheer joy of creation. Whether the soul's creations are such as to lead to fame and fortune depends on other features in the horoscope as well. The important point that the fifth house makes is that everyone has the power to create, and if you have the Sun in the fifth you will be made aware of that.

THE SIXTH HOUSE

As we learn to love, we desire to serve: first to serve those we love, and later, those we find less easy to love! Service is the keynote of the sixth house. Experiences in this house teach us that the path to divinity requires work and effort.

The sixth house is primarily concerned with the process of self-transmutation, with all those experiences that help to improve and alter the self for the better, gradually changing the imperfect and less desirable sides of ourselves (at whatever level) into a state of perfection. As with all processes of this nature, it takes a long time and requires what is best described by that old-fashioned word 'toil'. Thus, work of all descriptions comes under this house. For most of us this will mean our employment and those daily jobs and chores that we need to do to keep life going in an ordered way.

There is almost always an element of repetition and routine in this house, as the soul works away at some issue day after day, week after week. As White Eagle once said, it is not the occasional major experiences of life that enable us to do most of our growing, but those things we have to do again and again, 'the daily round, the common task', as the well known hymn has it. Thus any task that is repetitive or tedious is linked with this house, as is anything that requires us to be industrious, conscientious and exacting, especially with ourselves.

At heart, the sixth house and its corresponding sign, Virgo, are linked with what we can best understand through the ancient art of alchemy, that arcane process of transmuting base metal into gold. While it may be true that one or two alchemists did actually succeed in achieving this, the real point of the art is the metaphorical transmutation, that of our own 'base metals' into the true 'gold' of the spirit.

Any process like this requires that impurities and unwanted material or conditions are eliminated, which gives rise to the other major feature of life that is well known to be associated with this house: health. Ill health is, in effect, a process of eliminating impurities and inharmony within the soul that have, eventually, to be pushed out through the physical vehicle. People who have a strongly emphasized sixth house do not necessarily have health problems themselves, but are often drawn to work that involves health in some way, such as medicine, nutrition and diet, physical fitness and so on.

Being the house of service, the sixth also denotes those who serve us. Difficulties with employees, for example, may teach us important lessons about aspects of our own characters that require attention and improvement. Conditions might reflect past situations where the soul did not render service willingly or as well as it could; conversely, past loyal service may now bring the reward of faithful, hard working companions.

In short, in the sixth house we learn that God's plan is perfect. If we would be as God, as we all shall be one day, we must execute all life's tasks and processes perfectly, too. Then we shall indeed 'reap the golden harvest of the spirit'.

The Sun in the sixth house

If you have the Sun in the sixth house, the principle of service will play a large part in your day-to-day life. You may well be drawn to one of the 'service' professions. Involvement in medical fields such as nursing, pharmacology, nutrition and diet is common, or this may occur in the private life if, for example, you spend time caring for a sick relative or friend, or have to pay careful attention to your own health. Whether you find it pleasing or tiresome, the cultivation of 'a healthy mind in a healthy body' is important. There is often a tendency to anxiety: emphasis on Virgo (the corresponding sign) or the sixth house manifests itself as such a need to get things right that worrying is part and parcel of the process until the mind is really well controlled. 'Mind over matter' is a key point, and the general feeling of health and well-being is apt to be very easily affected by both mind and emotions – note that this can mean in a positive as well as a negative way.

The ruler of Virgo and the sixth house is the planet Mercury, reflecting the importance of mind as an agent of personal transmutation: as one thinks, so one becomes, as the ancients said. Just as in alchemy, the liquid metal mercury, which is able to dissolve most other metals, was the agent of transmutation in converting 'base metals' into gold, so, in our spiritual evolution, Mercury, or mind, is the agent of change and growth. If we learn nothing else in the sixth house, we learn sooner or later the importance of what we think – and how to change it, if that is necessary.

Because of the 'service' nature of the house, involvement with matters of employment is also common, as in personnel work, trade unions, industrial arbitration, pay review bodies, and health and safety issues. The Sun in the sixth is 'particular', and with good reason, although you may not necessarily like it. The soul is continually presented with situations that require this care over detail, the need to get everything exactly right. Others may say that this sometimes makes you difficult to live with, but this process of perfecting the self is part of everyone's experience at some point!

The need to be and to feel useful and worthwhile underlies almost all sixth-house manifestation, and it is rarely lazy; if the rest of the horoscope suggests a tendency to indolence, a sixth-house Sun works strongly against it. There can be a swing the other way, in that a person with this position tends to measure him- or herself, and often others too, by the amount of work done, or apparently done, but maturity brings a softer and less judgemental attitude, recognizing that ultimately the work without is but a reflection of the real work taking place within the soul, the constant effort towards self-improvement.

THE SEVENTH HOUSE

We have now reached the halfway point in our survey of the houses. From this point onwards, the remaining houses are each placed opposite one we have already discussed, and, as we shall see, opposing pairs of houses have a good deal in common, as well as being complementary.

The seventh house is placed opposite the first. Whereas the first house is the house of the self, the house through which the incarnating soul gathers to itself a physical body and personality, the seventh is the house of everyone else, very loosely speaking. In manifesting ourselves, we also find very soon that we affect the ability of others to manifest themselves, and they affect us likewise. Thus the seventh is the house that brings us experiences that teach us balance and compromise. An over-emphasized first house, being the house of the self, can sometimes make for a rather egocentric approach to life; with the seventh, this doesn't work. Seventh-house experience compels us to look outwards, not only to acknowledge the existence of others, but also their needs and rights, their value to society.

The seventh house always brings us up against 'the other person', and so is the house of almost all one-to-one situations. These include partnerships of all kinds, such as marriage and business partnerships, but also competitors, rivals and 'enemies'. It is through seventh-house experience that we seek to develop the qualities we lack, or those who can bring those qualities into our lives. Our competitors and rivals are so because they have or represent something that we lack or need to eliminate in ourselves. We are all familiar with the way in which certain individuals seem to reflect back at us things about ourselves that we do not necessarily feel happy about. This is a seventh-house experience, too.

The search for harmony in life is also intrinsic to the experiences of the seventh house. All these experiences, whatever their individual nature, have one aim: to help the soul to find true harmony, true accord with others, with one's surroundings, with all situations in life. Note, however, that this does not mean that the soul should be, or is, seeking the easy way. This is said often to be a fault associated with Libra, the

43

seventh and corresponding sign. In fact, the search for true harmony is hard work, whether in a marriage, a career, one's home or, in some circumstances, one's health, all ill health being ultimately a manifestation of inharmony at some level.

Not surprisingly, Venus is the planet most closely associated with the seventh house. The ideal of perfect harmony and accord with all is an obviously Venusian goal, but the effort required to reach this ideal gives the lie once and for all to any idea that Venus is the planet of the easy life. Venus, through the seventh house, demands a great deal of us. It presents us with experiences that compel us to develop flexibility, unselfishness, tact, diplomacy, poise, balance and objectivity, but also warmth of heart.

Because it is the house of 'other people', the seventh is also linked with our relations with the general public. People whose lives bring them before the public frequently have an emphasized seventh house. There are few better ways to learn about one's effect on others than through having, or choosing, to live a very public life!

The Sun in the seventh house
If you have the Sun in the seventh house, life will have made you very conscious of other people, even though

you may not always like having to be so. It takes the emphasis firmly away from oneself to others. There will often be one or two particular 'others', as in marriage or business partners; and there can also be a tendency to feel incomplete without a partner of some kind, even if the partnership to which your karma has drawn you is far from ideal. Better a difficult partnership than a solitary or unshared life, is usually the overriding feeling with a strong seventh.

As Venus is the planet associated with this house, it frequently accompanies creative and artistic ability. There may be a liking for appearing in public or showing one's work in public or, if one's karma is such that this is disliked, it happens anyway in order to draw the soul out beyond itself and its personal concerns.

Legal issues sometime arise with a strong seventh. Fairness and balance are always important, and a legal career may be chosen, or legal action embarked upon, in order to promote these qualities. Alternatively, you may find yourself on the other end of litigation or divorce proceedings.

It is only fair to say that many people with the Sun in the seventh go through life without any of this, but nevertheless the sense of justice is almost always very strong. If nothing else, this often makes for much argument and discussion. Sun in the seventh sometimes draws

45

people to politics, also to diplomatic work, because, at its best, this position denotes an acute conscious-ness of everyone's rights and needs. Many counsellors, arbitrators, troubleshooters and peacemakers have an emphasized seventh.

Ultimately, there is always a desire for harmony, even if others sometimes think that the process undertaken in order to reach it is anything but harmonious. Sun in the seventh can be argumentative, contentious, even litigious, but always with the aim of making things fair and, in the end, bringing harmony and peace. Conversely, there may sometimes be shyness and a seeming inability to exist independently of others, but this, too, is about moving away from self towards others, and seeking harmony through brotherhood with, at first, a few individuals, but eventually with all.

THE EIGHTH HOUSE

The eighth house, rather like its corresponding sign, Scorpio, has acquired a rather fearsome reputation among those who know a little, but not enough, about astrology. In medieval times, it was called the house of death, but this needs to be interpreted in the widest possible sense. What is really meant by this is probably best encapsulated in that famous goal known to Eastern religions as non-attachment.

The eighth house symbolizes all those experiences that help us to learn this hardest of lessons. It is very human to become attached to people, to things, to homes and environments, to possessions, to a job and so on, but with every one of these things there comes a time when they are no longer needed for our development. We need to move on to something new. The most obvious and, in a way, extreme example of this is provided by reincarnation. This enables us to start again with a new body and vehicles better adapted to what we need to learn and accomplish next. Without such opportunity, we would not be able to progress.

So, if we find that an eighth-house experience has taken something that we cherished away from us, we should try to realize that it will be replaced by something more suited to our 'next step' on the spiritual path. Some astrologers refer to the eighth as the house of transformation – a good term and much better than 'the house of death'! It is, indeed, through this house that we can be transformed.

The eighth is opposite the second, and this particular pairing exemplifies something we all have to learn at some stage in our growth: the need to balance the spiritual and material sides of life. As we have seen, the second represents the material side, but also the need to acquire the metaphorical materials for the building of the 'soul temple'. The eighth represents the spiritual side, the removal of anything that would spoil that temple or is not required for it, but also the help that may come from others, materially as well as spiritually, to assist the soul in its task. For this reason, the eighth is also the house of shared resources, such as the resources of the partner, or money lent or owing, legacies and so on. I realize this view of the eighth house as a source of help is not typical of the astrologers of the past, but it should be borne in mind by us all, especially those of us who openly profess an esoteric approach to astrology.

The eighth is also a house of temptation, because, through Scorpio, one of its rulers is Mars, the planet of the desire nature. Desire produces attachment, it is said; the eighth teaches non-attachment, but it can also do this by leading the soul to positions in which it has to choose between letting go of what it ought to let go, and grasping what it wants but does not actually need for its development. This is especially the case in power issues. Many of those with an emphasized eighth have to deal with karma associated with the use or misuse of power in past lives, with matters of domination, financial dealings, sexual issues and so on. However, the eighth is also the house of the real power that we all seek to develop: power over every aspect of ourselves, so that personality becomes merely a tool that the soul can use on its path to enlightenment.

The Sun in the eighth house

If you have the Sun in the eighth house you will have had to become used to a life of very intense experience, even if that experience is mostly hidden from others. This position does not allow the soul to 'skate on the surface of life', to ignore what lies within, and brings a number

49

of situations into the life that force a confrontation with the problems that need to be dealt with. Avoidance is seldom possible: the confrontation is emphatic and definite, calling forth inner resources – resources that often one didn't realize one had until then.

Because of the need to let go that is so much highlighted by this house, leaving things behind, saying goodbye, sacrificing or giving away certain things, whether literally or metaphorically, is common and often frequent in the life. For example, it may lead to involvement in circumstances connected with death and dying, such as work in hospitals and hospices, undertaking, dealing with wills and legacies and so on, or simply dealing internally with the aftermath of bereavement.

There is often a need to share resources with others, or to seek help from them, which may require one's pride to be pocketed or a display of openness that is personally disliked and unwanted; privacy is nearly always preferred. Unless the rest of the horoscope dictates otherwise, the emotions are usually very strong and can take a long time to control.

However, because this, above all the houses, is the one that confronts the soul with inner crises, those with the Sun in the eighth often come into their own in times of external crisis. They often make good surgeons and paramedics, for example. Like those in the opposite house, the second, eighth-house people are often drawn to financial work, which may bring temptations from which the soul learns much. They often thrive on living 'on the edge', whether this be physically or metaphorically.

Being linked with what tends to be inward and hidden, the eighth is also the house associated with occult matters; the soul may be drawn to such things or be frightened of them, according to karma, but 'inner' issues cannot be ignored. Occasionally, then, this position leads to clairvoyance or mediumship.

The ultimate tests associated with the Sun in the eighth are always ones of power. Financial and sexual temptations are common, so is the temptation simply to misuse or abuse a position of power in some way. The eighth can be very manipulative, and evolved indeed is the eighth-house person who can truly let go of personal desire (as symbolized by Mars, co-ruler of this house), surrendering all to the greater good. The eighth denotes forces that can work strongly for both good and ill; the test for the soul living with them is to be able to control them and use them selflessly, a hard task indeed, but tremendously well worth doing!

THE NINTH HOUSE

After the intense trials and efforts associated with the eighth house, it is perhaps with some relief that we turn now to the ninth. Readers who know something about astrology might think the ninth is very different from the eighth, but the two do have one important thing in common: they both include types of experience that could be described as investigative. Both stimulate the soul to 'look into' things. In the eighth house, there is a desire to find out what's really going on underneath life's surface, a desire to get at the truth within. In the ninth, the soul is led to experiences that are designed to expand the consciousness. It operates chiefly through the mental body, unlike the eighth, which works largely through the emotions.

Since expansion of consciousness is the keynote, the ninth, like its corresponding sign, Sagittarius, is inevitably linked with such matters as higher education, philosophy, religion, any experiences involving other countries and customs, long-distance travel (including space travel), invention and so on. Jupiter is the ruler of both the sign and house, and is the planet that most represents the growing consciousness of humanity.

The position of the ninth house in the horoscope wheel is itself of interest: it falls in the 'early afternoon' position, just after the peak of midday (represented by the mid-heaven). Although nowadays many of us seem to be born with a desire to expand the consciousness, often in life it is only after the completion of worldly achievements (mid-heaven/tenth house) that we begin to think about what lies beyond 'ordinary' life. In turn, a deeper and wider understanding developed in the ninth both catalyses and gives us the wherewithal to deal with the transformational processes of the eighth.

If it is true – as it surely is – that 'as a man thinks, so he becomes', the ninth can provide very powerful tools for self-improvement and evolution. Appropriately, it falls opposite the third house, the house of general and taken-for-granted mental activity, and just as the third is linked with Gemini, the third sign, the ninth is linked with the expansive and freedom-loving Sagittarius. While the third is all about communication in a routine way, the ninth is about long-distance communication, both physically and in the sense of communication with those higher forces and levels of life that lie behind human growth and consciousness.

Because both the third and ninth operate so strongly at the mental level, oppositions across these houses tend to indicate much restlessness, which often takes considerable effort and strength of will to calm and focus. The boredom threshold is usually very low, and there is a tendency to wander from one thing to another, the key being, of course, to keep the mind thoroughly occupied!

Ninth-house experiences are, in essence, all part of the soul's quest for enlightenment. Some of us might pursue that quest more consciously and vigorously than others, but for every one of us the quest is there somewhere. If the ninth is heavily tenanted, then it is particularly important in the current life.

The Sun in the ninth house

If you have the Sun in the ninth house, the chances are that you will end your life a long way from where you started it. Sometimes this is literal, manifesting as relocation abroad, perhaps more than once; sometimes it is more metaphorical, indicating a journey of the mind and spirit. Changes in religious belief and attitude are common. Typically, a ninth-house person is brought up in, or at least influenced by, a particular religion in childhood but later 'rebels' against it, asserting an independence of soul that seeks its own path.

This is the position of the traveller, and, in concert with the well known saying 'it is better to travel hopefully than to arrive', the journey often seems more important than the goal. A great variety of experience is usually sought deliberately, although karmic circumstances can sometimes lead to a life in which the person seems an unwilling participant in the irregular changes and translocations that are typical of the Sun in the ninth.

The greatest challenge with this position is to overcome restlessness, both physical and mental, and to learn to focus and concentrate. The key is keeping the mind occupied and, in youth, the body as well. Unless karma dictates otherwise, plenty of physical activity is very usual – this is typically a 'sporty' house. It is also the house of activities such as long-distance walking, exploration, equestrian pursuits and 'the great outdoors' generally. At the mental level, this position sometimes leads to an academic career, and frequently to a career in one of the professions, particularly education or the law. Work connected with travel is also common, especially shipping or air travel.

As the ninth is the house of long-distance and mass communication, involvement in the media is also common – radio and television, information technology and so on. Work in scientific research is also typical.

Because the ninth is the house of ethics and standards, philosophy and religion, these areas, too, are important, and in later life people with this position often find themselves advising and guiding others. The travel of their earlier years, as it were, leads them to act as a travel guide to others on the one journey that really matters: the journey of life itself.

Generally speaking, the ninth-house person seems to lead a more 'interesting' life than that of someone in almost any other position, with both the advantages and drawbacks that might be expected from that!

THE TENTH HOUSE

In marked contradistinction to the ninth, the tenth house ties us firmly to earth. However, as with other pairs of next-door houses, the tenth and ninth share a common attribute, in this case aspiration. This is very appropriate, as the boundary common to the two houses is the mid-heaven, the highest point in the chart. Ninth-house aspirations are directed to abstract goals as a rule, whereas those of the tenth are generally very definite and concrete, and usually concern the career or vocation.

The tenth has often been described as indicating the 'work in the world', which is not a bad description. Among other things, it serves to highlight the importance of what we actually do. Service is a major keynote of human life, and most of us accomplish much of our service through our 'work in the world'.

The tenth is also important with respect to how others see us. Since we tend to judge people according to 'what they do', that is their careers, this is not surprising. In some circumstances, and certainly in the working sphere, tenth-house conditions are the ones that others will notice even above the ascendant and first house, which operate much more obviously in the personal life.

The mid-heaven, which is, of course, the cusp of the tenth house, traditionally represents the summit of achievement, the highest it is possible to attain. Thus it denotes the position someone can reach in life, in terms of both professional promotion and social standing. The latter is not regarded as a 'politically correct' subject in present times, but is nevertheless still very much a reality. Whether we like it or not, a hierarchy exists in almost all areas of life, and one's place in that hierarchy will generally be found to be linked with tenth-house conditions in general, and the mid-heaven in particular.

Because of this, the tenth is also associated with one's parentage and ancestry. This clearly links it with its opposite house, the fourth, the house of home and family. It is usually said that each of these houses represents one of the parents, although not always the same way round. Usually the tenth-house parent is the one that has the most obvious outward effect on the life. The term 'parentage' can also be taken metaphorically, indicating the experience that has been gathered by the soul in previous incarnations to enable it to occupy its present-day position and role in life.

Tenth-house experience can vary as widely as the types of career and work we pursue, but one thing will always follow such experience eventually, even if only after many lives: a dawning understanding that worldly aspiration and effort can only achieve so much, and that our true role in life is service, not simply to ourselves and others, but, above all, to God, that divine source from which we were all breathed forth in the beginning. Sooner or later, the trials and tribulations we meet through the tenth bring us to the point where we have to kneel in humility and call upon a higher force for help and understanding. Then the soul's true role in life is understood, and the possibilities for achievement are no longer limited. Pride in the achievements of the self is replaced by humility and a joyful participation in the achievements of God working through the self.

The Sun in the tenth house

If you have the Sun in the tenth house, life is likely to challenge you to strive for greater achievement, whatever your 'position' in life. Career issues frequently, although not invariably, predominate, and if the rest of the horoscope concurs, a long-term effort will eventually lead to success, albeit not necessarily in the way at first envisaged. The corresponding sign, Capricorn, has a gift that is unusual in humankind: patience. This is associated with the ruler of both sign and house, Saturn. While the tenth house does not always call forth this quality, it generally does so if the soul feels that the goal being worked towards is a worthwhile one. Success rarely comes early in life with this position; it has to be worked for, but steady application and effort bring later rewards.

There can be a tendency to identify oneself with one's career, which can cause problems later when retirement looms, but irrespective of this, the person with Sun in the tenth can become a real authority in his or her field, and may be called upon for assistance well beyond any artificial retirement age. If karma, or chosen circumstance, dictates that there is no career in the usual sense, some other occupation in life becomes a substitute for it, and just the same growth to a position of 'authority' is likely.

The other major area of life in which the Sun in the tenth tends to be felt is in family matters, especially those involving heredity, ancestry and 'class' issues. The tenth appropriately falls opposite the fourth, the house of the domestic life, and, like the fourth, emphasizes family matters. However, while the fourth is about the private life, the tenth is about the public side of one's family life. Those with the Sun in the tenth are often acutely conscious of their position, social or professional, and may need to watch that their attention is focused on real goals rather than on 'the climb to the top'. Unlike in the ninth house, where the journey is more important than the goal, in the tenth it is definitely the other way round: the goal matters most. In certain individual cases this can lead to an attitude that considers the end to justify the means, but sooner or later life corrects this.

Ultimately, the Sun in the tenth is all about the importance of using our gifts and talents to serve both God and humanity; those with this position are at their best when doing exactly that.

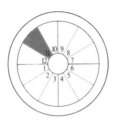

THE ELEVENTH HOUSE

In medieval times, astrologers referred to the eleventh
house as the house of hopes, wishes and ideals. In many
ways this is a very apt, although not complete, description, expressing very succinctly the forward-looking,
idealistic and aspirational types of experience one readily links with Aquarius, the corresponding sign. As we
stand on the threshold of the 'age of Aquarius', this
house is perhaps of special interest. Many of those who
are at the forefront of humanitarian, ecological and
spiritual enterprises have this house emphasized. Along
with the ninth, this is the most forward-looking, the
most future-oriented of the houses.

While its experiences can be very challenging, as
one would expect they are frequently very inspiring too
– somehow this is a house that helps to bring out the
best in us all. It presents us with situations that require

us to rise to the occasion, to be unselfish, and above all to be prepared to work with others towards a common goal. The eleventh is the house of teamwork, and is not a place of solitary experience, unlike the twelfth (of which more later). In the eleventh, we learn to join hands with others, and this can happen in a myriad of different ways.

Note that this house is linked with the element air, and, like the other two airy houses, the third and the seventh, it covers experiences in human relationships. Astrologers recognize it as the house of friends and associates in the widest sense, including groups of people, societies, and ultimately one's relations with the wider world as a whole.

It sits, appropriately, opposite the fifth house. The latter is the house of the heart, linked with some of the most intimate of human experiences. The eleventh, on the other hand, requires that what has been learned intimately about the nature and power of love is put into practice with many others, as the soul is led to situations that require it to recognize and acknowledge the love of God in the hearts of us all, and thereby truly to join with others in brotherhood and shared endeavour.

The difficulties that can sometimes be associated with this house generally result from a tendency to over-idealism, lack of practicality and, sometimes, thinking that is either too way-out or too fixed. It is the role of the house, however, to bring to the soul experiences that help it to overcome these very problems. It is perhaps in the realm of thought that the greatest tests come; those with a strong eleventh often find they have to learn just how powerful thoughts can be, and thus to be careful what they think!

If you wish to sum up the eleventh house in one word, let that word be 'humanity'. The best of the house manifests in sheer humanity, both in the sense that it encourages the equal and compassionate treatment of all and in the sense that it imparts an understanding of what it means to be a human being.

The Sun in the eleventh house

If you have the Sun in the eleventh house you will be naturally inclined to optimism, to looking forward, however difficult life may be. It is rare to find an eleventh-house person who lacks ideals, however unusual or difficult to realize these may be. Such ideals are always in the mind's eye of the person with the Sun in the eleventh house, drawing him or her on through life's experiences towards fulfilment.

This is generally a sociable house, and Sun in the eleventh has many friends and associates, although with one important proviso: these people prefer to keep their friends, or most of them, at a certain distance. Unlike its opposite house, the eleventh is not one for great intimacy, tending to keep relationships on as rational and unemotional a footing as possible. Obviously, this does not preclude the normal intimate relationships of life with such people as partners and children, but in the outside world the soul is much more comfortable without a lot of emotion, perhaps recognizing that this would cloud its vision. The greater good matters more than the well-being of individuals, although these people are often very good at friendship and can usually be relied upon to be loyal and honest companions.

The eleventh is very much the house of teamwork and group enterprise, meaning that the needs of the individual are subsumed by those of the group. This may be the soul's natural inclination, but sometimes the Sun here denotes a karmic condition that the soul has imposed upon itself to make it pay more attention to the needs and goals of the wider world than to personal preoccupations.

The 'old' ruler of Aquarius and the eleventh is Saturn, and there is sometimes a need to break out of old, fixed, conservative attitudes in order to develop flexibility of mind and a new vision. The 'new' ruler is Uranus, which represents, above all, truth. Aquarius and the eleventh house are both concerned with the search for truth; the eleventh brings to the soul experiences that help it to find that truth, as well as opportunities to join with others to help humanity by sharing its burdens. It is about making 'a new heaven and a new earth', in however small or large a way. At the very least, Sun in the eleventh encourages co-operation with others and a more altruistic approach to life. At its best, it believes that any ideal is possible to realize, and will often go a long way towards proving that to be the case.

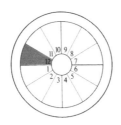

THE TWELFTH HOUSE

When we turn to the twelfth house, it might seem that the contrast could not be greater. This, the last house, perhaps demands more effort to understand than any of the others. Whereas the eleventh house is all about teamwork, the twelfth is about the work that we all have to do within ourselves, often very privately. Solitude is often necessary. The one thing the two houses do have in common is their aspiration. In the eleventh, the aspirations are generally shared with many others openly; in the twelfth lies the greatest aspiration of all: to reach God, to return to the divine source from which we were once breathed forth. This aspiration is shared by many others as well, but often not openly.

The twelfth was once called 'the house of self-undoing'. Again, this is not wrong, but it does perhaps give rather too dire an impression of the nature of twelfth-house experience. It is true that some of the experiences we would regard as the most difficult in a worldly sense belong here, but when we understand what lies behind them, we can take a rather different view. For example, suppose we consider someone who is confined to hospital with a chronic and serious illness, a typical twelfth-house situation. We may see, or think we see, very great suffering. However, could we but see behind the earthly condition, we might see a soul that has deliberately chosen to undergo this experience to purge itself of some inharmony and thus free it from some past karmic tie so that it can move forward in joy and freedom. Similarly, many of those who are imprisoned, literally or metaphorically, have somewhere along the line chosen to be in that position so that they can work on faults and defects of character, which, having been rectified, then lead the soul to a freedom it could not have found in any other way. Voluntary seclusion and solitude are frequently sought by the twelfth-house type of character in order to think, to work on problems, to purify and transform the self so that the soul may grow nearer to God.

From all this it may be concluded that the real purpose of twelfth-house experience is to eliminate all those things that might be standing in the way of the soul's path back to God and therefore to ultimate freedom.

True, the experiences may be hard and bitter, and they may also be so private that no one else knows about them, but the reward for success, however long it takes to achieve, is the greatest reward of all: consciousness of God, cosmic consciousness, divine bliss, call it what you will.

Yes, the twelfth is the house of self-undoing because it ruthlessly exposes our weaknesses and imperfections, but by so doing, it enables us to deal with and rise above them so that we may truly dwell in the glory of God. Thus, the circle that began with the ascendant, the point at which the glory of the Sun is revealed, returns to that same point, but now it is a yet more glorious sunrise, crowned by experience and, in the end, a total surrender to and blending with the divine source that the Sun symbolizes.

The Sun in the twelfth house

If you have the Sun in the twelfth house, you will have found that most of life's really important experiences have been met inwardly and usually secretly, others very seldom being aware of them. Childhood is often difficult or unusual with this position, and there are frequently peculiarities or defects in the early family life that, although often taken in their stride by these people, would seem very abnormal to others. These can range from the most lurid 'skeletons in the family cupboard' to a chronically sick or absent parent or other close family member. Physical isolation or seclusion is common, and those with this position often find themselves thrown back upon their own resources, psychologically if not in any other way.

Quite frequently, such seclusion or isolation is deliberately sought in later life in order to gain space for deep contemplation and assimilation of experience. Twelfth-house experience tends to come at the end of a particular karmic cycle, when all sorts of 'loose ends' are being tied up and the soul is clearing out everything that might be in the way or not needed for the next cycle. The twelfth triggers a kind of psychic spring-clean, a cleansing and purifying process that has to be undergone before the next step forward can be taken.

Jupiter and Neptune are the natural rulers of the twelfth house and its corresponding sign, Pisces. Both planets seek to expand and raise consciousness, so the twelfth is also closely linked with spiritual and religious experience; indeed, it can lead to a religious life. Above all, through the twelfth we seek to express the glory of God, which may seem strange for a house that often appears to impose so many privations and difficulties. This is not the paradox it seems, however: the twelfth is about clearing away all those things that stand between us and God, leading to an ever more perfect expression of God in our lives.

Thus, it is also common to find great creativity in those with the Sun in the twelfth. It may lead to a career in the arts, especially drama. Marine careers are also associated with the Sun in the twelfth, whether in the forces, science or travel. As with the ninth house, there is often an interest in space and, indeed, anything limitless in which the soul can 'lose itself'. Careers in which the soul is a tiny cog in a very large machine are also common, such as a secretary in a huge multinational company. This is because this type of experience teaches us humility through insignificance, but also because we are part of a great whole – ultimately that oneness that the word 'universe' symbolizes.

APPENDIX: CALCULATING THE POSITION OF YOUR SOLAR HOUSE

Most of us know which sign of the zodiac our Sun sign is, but probably very few know which house in our horoscope the Sun is placed in. Below are some instructions to enable you to work this out.

First, as well as the date and place of your birth, you need to know as accurately as possible what time you were born. If you do not know, there are various ways to find out.

For example, if you were born in hospital, it will have been recorded on your records, and provided that those for your year of birth have not yet been destroyed, you will be able to obtain the information. Other family members are always worth asking; although they may not be completely accurate, they can often be right within about half an hour if they do remember the occasion. Sometimes the time of births is recorded in family diaries or bibles. Nowadays, many countries record the time as well as the date and place of birth on birth certificates. This happens in, for example, the USA, much of continental Europe, and Scotland. The time of birth of twins is almost always certified on all documents in case matters arise subsequently that require proof of which is the elder twin.

If you still 'draw a blank', don't despair! When you read this book, you may be able to identify for yourself the house that 'feels' right.

If day and night were always of equal length, the next stage would be simple. You would simply divide the twenty-four hours of the day into twelve two-hour segments, and the house would be determined by these. If you were born close to the equator, this does actually apply, although there are still some approximations involved if the place of your birth was at a somewhat different longitude from the standard time used in that country. However, at this stage we won't worry about that, but simply set out the basic times and houses for a rough calculation for birth near the equator (Table 1).

Generally speaking, if you were born in the central hour of these periods, near the equator, Table 1 will give an accurate result. If you were born within half an hour of a change of house, according to slight variations in sunrise and sunset at different times of year (even on the equator these vary by half an hour over a whole year) and longitude differences, you could have the Sun in

Table 1: The approximate position of the Sun throughout the day near the equator

Time of birth	Position of the Sun
Midnight–2am	Third house
2–4am	Second house
4–6am	First house
6–8am	Twelfth house
8–10am	Eleventh house
10am–noon	Tenth house
Noon–2pm	Ninth house
2–4pm	Eighth house
4–6pm	Seventh house
6–8pm	Sixth house
8–10pm	Fifth house
10pm–midnight	Fourth house

the next or previous house. When you read the descriptions in the book, it will usually be very obvious which is right. If it isn't obvious, this probably means that you have important celestial bodies in both houses.

If your place of birth was outside the tropics, additional rules need to be applied, as the length of day and night varies according to season, but even so, with a little careful, simple calculation, you can still arrive at an answer that, like the equatorial table above, is correct to within one house either side.

First, find out the times of sunrise and sunset at your place of birth on the day of the year on which you were born. This will be the same each year, so the current year's times will do – if you were born in a capital city you can sometimes find these in desk diaries, as well as in annual almanacs or on the internet.

Now – and this is perhaps the trickiest bit! – work out the amount of time that elapses on this day for the two main periods of the day: sunrise to sunset; and sunset to sunrise. Then divide each of these into six equal periods. For example, if the sun rises at 6.45am and sets at 4.45pm, those ten hours will divide into six periods of one hundred minutes each: 6.45–8.25am, 8.25–10.05am, 10.05–11.45am, 11.45am to 1.25pm, 1.25–3.05pm, and 3.05–4.45pm. Similarly, the night half – fourteen hours – will divide into six periods of one hundred and forty minutes: 4.45–7.05pm, 7.05–9.25pm, 9.25–11.45pm, 11.45pm to 2.05am, 2.05–4.25am, and 4.25–6.45am. Each of these periods corresponds to the Sun being in the (day) twelfth, eleventh, tenth, ninth, eighth and seventh houses, or (night) sixth, fifth, fourth, third, second and first houses, respectively.

Remember when applying your own birth time to this table to deduct first any 'summer time' or 'daylight saving time' that would have applied. Thus, if you were born at 9.10am according to the clock during a period when daylight saving was in operation, your actual 'standard' birth time is 8.10am.

All this may sound a bit involved, but the underlying principles are relatively straightforward. If you find it too arduous, see if you can persuade a relative or friend to work it out for you.

THE WHITE EAGLE
SCHOOL OF ASTROLOGY

The White Eagle School of Astrology, of which the author of this book is the current principal, is part of the White Eagle Lodge's 'Wisdom School'. It runs correspondence courses in astrology, and occasional 'live' courses, lectures and retreats. The correspondence courses, which are recognised by the Advisory Panel on Astrological Education, lead to a diploma qualification.

For further information about the school and its courses, please visit our website:

www.whiteagleastrology.org

Or you can write to us at:
New Lands, Brewells Lane, Liss
Hampshire, GU33 7HY
England

Or e-mail us at:
astrology@whiteagle.org

You can telephone us on:
01730-893300 (international: +44-1730-893300)

LEARNING ABOUT ASTROLOGY

A major part of the work of the White Eagle School of Astrology is the teaching of astrology. Much of this is aimed specifically at those who want either to develop a working knowledge of the subject or to become professional. However, we also cater for those who simply want to engage with the subject and feel unable, or disinclined, to deal with the technicalities and processes of study involved in conventional courses.

We have run correspondence courses for many years. Indeed, when Joan Hodgson, founder of the school, initiated the beginners' course in 1941, it was the only such course available in the UK. This course, which has undergone revision roughly once a decade since then, continues to run to this day.

For those who have already learned some astrology elsewhere and wish to 'switch' to our approach, there is a preparatory course, which comprises the second half of the beginners' course.

An advanced course leading to a diploma was published in the early 1970s. It, too, with regular revision, continues to run.

The great advantage of correspondence courses is, of course, that they can be taken anywhere at any time. The disadvantage is the lack of 'live' teaching.

For those who feel they need live teaching, from time to time we run intensive residential courses at New Lands, and occasionally elsewhere. We also hold occasional astrology 'days', and these are usually accessible for all levels of ability.

The White Eagle Publishing Trust, which publishes and distributes the White Eagle teaching, is part of the wider work of the White Eagle Lodge, a 'wisdom school' for the present age, in which people may find a place for growth and understanding, and where the teachings of White Eagle find practical expression. Here, men and women may come to learn the reason for their life on earth and how to serve and live in harmony with the whole brotherhood of life, visible and invisible, in health and happiness. The White Eagle Publishing Trust website is at:

www.whiteaglepublishing.org

Readers wishing to know more about the work of the White Eagle Lodge may contact us as follows.

You can visit our websites at:
www.whiteagle.org (worldwide)
www.whiteaglelodge.org (Americas)
www.whiteeaglelodge.org.au (Australasia)
www.whiteagleca.com (Canada)

You can e-mail us at:
enquiries@whiteagle.org (worldwide)
sjrc@whiteaglelodge.org (Americas)
enquiries@whiteeaglelodge.org.au (Australasia)

You can write to us at:
The White Eagle Lodge
New Lands
Brewells Lane
Liss
Hampshire
GU33 7HY
England
Tel: 01730-893300

The Church of the White Eagle Lodge
PO Box 930
Montgomery
Texas 77356
USA
Tel: 936-597-5757

The White Eagle Lodge (Australasia)
PO Box 225
Maleny
Queensland 4552
Australia
Tel: 07-5494-4169

OTHER BOOKS PUBLISHED BY THE WHITE EAGLE PUBLISHING TRUST

ASTROLOGY, THE SACRED SCIENCE:
A SPIRITUAL PERSPECTIVE

BY JOAN HODGSON

Astrology the Sacred Science is a visionary book, in which astrology is used to describe the individual's path to perfect awareness, both on earth and at a spiritual level. Written in understandable terms, it is a book about human destiny and the great cycles of creation, but also about applying the principle of love in daily life.

Chapters include 'The human body and the heavens', 'The seven rays of unfoldment', and 'The soul lessons of each element and zodiac sign'. In addition, there is information on the great ages, both past and those to come. This multilayered book can serve as an introduction to spiritual astrology, as well as offering an enlightening approach to the experienced astrologer.

21.6 x 13.8cm, 234 + xviii pp, diagrams, pbk.
ISBN 978-0-85487-046-2

WISDOM IN THE STARS

BY JOAN HODGSON

The astrology of this book is esoteric – that is, astrology at the deeper level of soul and spirit. Read this book to discover things about your Sun sign beyond anything you will find in most of the available literature about the zodiac. In addition, rediscover aspects of your life that will enable you to change and grow with confidence through inner powers that are specific to your sign.

17.6 x 11.0cm, 117 + xi pp, pbk.
ISBN 978-0-85487-159-4

PLANETARY HARMONIES:
AN ASTROLOGICAL BOOK OF MEDITATION

BY JOAN HODGSON

The opening of the chakras is a key aspect of spiritual enlightenment, as has been shown by Eastern spiritual traditions. In this book, Joan gives a whole new account of these, the colours associated with them and their place in spiritual unfoldment. She also brings East and West together by using meditation practices from the Essenes, as well as from her own intuition based on White Eagle's teaching and esoteric astrology. Joan gives meditations for each of the full and new moons, linking them with the signs of the zodiac, as well as inspiring readers to look further into this area. This is a book for study and contemplation, as well as meditation, with a universal appeal. Chapters include: 'The way of meditation', 'Thought-control', 'The four elements', 'Meditations for the days of the week', 'The planets and the planes of consciousness in meditation'.

21.6 x 13.8cm, 145 + xv pp, illustrated, hdbk.
ISBN 978-0-85487-081-3